A CULTURAL HISTORY OF WOMEN IN AMERICA

STRENGTH IN NUMBERS: INDUSTRIALIZATION AND POLITICAL ACTIVISM 1861–1899

CATH SENKER

CHELSEA HOUSE
An Infobase Learning Company

STRENGTH IN NUMBERS: INDUSTRIALIZATION AND POLITICAL ACTIVISM 1861–1899

Copyright © 2011 Bailey Publishing Associates Ltd

Produced for Chelsea House by Bailey Publishing Associates Ltd, 11a Woodlands, Hove BN3 6TJ, England

Library of Congress Cataloging-in-Publication Data
Senker, Cath.
 Strength in numbers : industrialization and political activism, 1861-1899 / Cath Senker.
   p. cm. — (A cultural history of women in America)
Includes index.
ISBN 978-1-60413-931-0
1. Women—United States--Social conditions—19th century—Juvenile literature. 2. Feminism—United States—History—19th century—Juvenile literature. 3. Women's rights—United States—History—19th century—Juvenile literature. 4. United States—Social conditions—1865–1918—Juvenile literature. I. Title. II. Series.
HQ1419.S44 2011
305.420973'09034—dc22

                    2010045964

Project management by Patience Coster
Text design by Jane Hawkins
Picture research by Shelley Noronha
Printed and bound in Malaysia
Bound book date: April 2011

10 9 8 7 6 5 4 3 2 1 3386

This book is printed on acid-free paper.

All links and Web addresses were checked and verified to be correct at the time of publication. Because of the dynamic nature of the Web, some addresses and links may have changed since publication and may no longer be valid.

The publishers would like to thank the following for permission to reproduce their pictures:
Jane Addams Hull-House Photographic Collection: 49 (University of Illinois at Chicago Library, Special Collections); akg/North Wind Picture Archives: 59; The Art Archive: 5 (Culver Pictures), 9 (Culver Pictures), 17 (Culver Pictures), 30, 31 (National Archives, Washington, D.C.), 39 (Erin Pauwels Collection), 45 (Private Collection MD), 54 (Art Institute of Chicago/Superstock); The Bridgeman Art Library: 10 (Peter Newark Pictures), 20 (Christie's Images), 47 (Peter Newark Pictures); Corbis: 15 (Bettmann), 18 (Andy Kingsbury), 24 (Bettmann), 27, 33 (Bettmann), 37 (Bettmann), 38, 50 (Bettmann), 51, 52 (Bettmann); Getty Images: 7, 8, 11, 12, 16, 19, 21, 29, 32, 36, 42, 44, 48, 58; Lebrecht Music & Arts/North Wind: 23, 28, 46; The Library of Congress: 14, 35; TopFoto/The Granger Collection: 6, 13, 22, 25, 26, 34, 40, 41, 43, 53, 55, 56, 57.

CONTENTS

IN 1861, MOST WOMEN IN AMERICA WORKED hard as housewives, caring for their home and family. Yet the situation of women depended greatly on their class and race and where they lived in the United States. This book looks at the varied experiences of women in the late 19th century.

The Industrial Revolution began during the early 19th century with the development of the factory system. Industrialization brought new opportunities for white women to work outside the home, as textile workers, for example. Black women were denied these options; most African-American women were slaves working on white farms.

By 1861, a growing abolitionist movement was fighting to end the injustice of slavery.

Many women abolitionists joined the growing movement for women's rights too. Reforms earlier in the century had given women a little more control over their lives. For example, the Married Women's Property Act (1848) allowed married women to keep property they owned before marriage. Some girls, mostly white, were benefiting from the increasing availability of education for females. Yet women still did not have the right to vote. Most were subject to the will of their father or husband and had little say about their own future.

Right: A housewife washing the dishes in the kitchen of her tenement apartment in New York, 1905. In the late 1800s and early 1900s, tenements had no running water.

"

OVERWORKED

"We are told that the women of America have much leisure time but I haven't yet met any woman who thought so! Here the mistress of the house must do all the work that the cook, the maid, and the housekeeper would do in an upper-class family at home. Moreover, she must do her work as well as these three together do it in Norway."

From a letter to her parents, written by Norwegian immigrant Gro Svendsen in 1862. She thought American women had to work extremely hard to keep their homes in good order.

CHAPTER I

SURVEY OF THE ERA

T HE ABSENCE OF THEIR MENFOLK DURING THE AMERICAN CIVIL WAR meant that women took on new roles and responsibilities at home and in the field of battle. The introduction of laws after the war drew attention not only to the issue of slavery but also to the unequal way in which women were treated. The Industrial Revolution and large-scale migration in search of work also transformed women's lives.

CIVIL WAR

In the late 1850s, disputes between the northern and southern states over slavery, trade, and states' rights came to a head. The northern states opposed the extension of slavery to the new territories of the West. However, the economy of the southern states depended on it; southern leaders feared that the restriction of slavery would destroy their way of life. In 1860, after Abraham Lincoln won the presidential election, the southern states seceded (left the Union) to become the Confederate States of America, under President Jefferson Davis. In 1861, civil war broke out between the Union and the Confederacy. In 1865, the Union forces won. As a result of the war, the states were reunited and slavery was abolished.

Below: When the Civil War ended, the freed slaves were allowed to go to school for the first time. As shown in this illustration of a classroom in New York City in 1870, they were taught in segregated, black-only schools.

RECONSTRUCTION

From 1865 to 1877, a process called Reconstruction took place, during which government was re-established over the entire United States. New laws were introduced. The 13th Amendment of 1865 abolished slavery, while the 14th Amendment of 1868 gave black people citizenship and equal legal and civil rights. Under the 15th Amendment of 1870, all citizens had voting rights—but women were not included. The Reconstruction Acts forced all the southern states rejoining the Union to accept these laws and give civil rights to freed slaves.

Despite the end of slavery, black people's economic situation changed little. From 1877, the southern states brought in new laws to discriminate against black people and prevent them from achieving equal rights. The laws required separate public facilities, such as schools and transportation, for whites and non-whites.

THE EXPANSION OF INDUSTRY

During Reconstruction and after, the Industrial Revolution rapidly gained momentum. Between the late 1870s and the late 1890s, the volume of industrial production and the number of industrial workers doubled. The iron and steel industries expanded at an even greater rate. The annual production of steel rocketed from about 1.4 million tons in 1880 to more than 11 million tons in 1900. An assortment of inventions, including the electric light, the automobile, and the

Left: This painting by Charles Graham (1852–1911) depicts workers processing pig iron in a factory in Birmingham, Alabama, around 1890.

> **LIBERTY FOR ALL**
>
> "To-day, out of the din and smoke of the conflict, through anguish and misery unutterable, the nation has been brought to feel sympathy for the right, and reverence [respect] for justice. If black men are given a chance to save themselves, they will save us. Let these men earn their liberty, and they will secure everlastingly the liberty of the nation."
>
> Abolitionist Anna Dickinson was a popular public speaker for the Union during the Civil War. This excerpt is from her 1863 speech "How God Is Teaching the Nation."

TURNING POINT

THE 15TH AMENDMENT

Women later quoted the 15th Amendment, arguing that it should include women as voters because they were citizens. The text of the amendment stated: "The right of citizens of the United States to vote shall not be denied or abridged [limited] by the United States or by any State on account of race, color, or previous condition of servitude [slavery]. . . . The Congress shall have power to enforce this article by appropriate legislation."

WHITE WARMONGERS

"The Piutes, and other tribes west of the Rocky Mountains, are not fond of going to war. I never saw a wardance but once. It is always the whites that begin the wars, for their own selfish purposes. The government does not take to send the good men; there are a plenty who would take pains to see and understand the chiefs and learn their characters, and their good will to the whites. But the whites have not waited to find out how good the Indians were."

In 1883, Native American Sarah Winnemucca described how her people, the Paiutes, did not want to go to war, but the Europeans were determined to wage war against them.

Above: At the Battle of the Little Big Horn, Montana, in 1876, the Sioux and Cheyenne slaughtered General George Custer and his men. However, U.S. troops subsequently poured into the region and defeated the Native Americans.

telephone, sparked new industries. Railroads were constructed to transport goods and people around the country. Several innovations improved the home lives of those who could afford them. The increased use of electric power and gaslight in the home meant people relied less on candlelight. Indoor plumbing provided water direct to the house, while using a sewing machine sped up the process of making and mending clothes and soft furnishings.

The fast pace of technological development transformed the economy, yet progress was not smooth. The economy swung regularly from boom to slump; a long depression occurred from 1873 to 1878. Hostility between business owners and the new industrial working class led to the creation of national labor unions, set up to defend workers' conditions. Strikes took place during the depression of the mid-1870s and again in 1886.

MOVING WEST

Another way working people tried to better their situation was through migration. During the second half of the 19th century, large numbers of Europeans moved to the western territories acquired by the United States from Mexico after the end of the Mexican–American War (1848).

The migrants enjoyed great economic opportunities, but their arrival had a devastating effect on the Native American and Mexican people in the region. There were wars over land between Native Americans and settlers.

AN INFLUX OF MIGRANTS

During the last two decades of the 19th century, more than nine million people migrated to the United States. The majority came from northern or western Europe. They sought land for farming or jobs in the growing cities. Migrants were generally paid lower wages than native-born Americans and suffered from discrimination and bad treatment. Yet they contributed greatly to their new homeland. In addition to their labor, the newcomers brought their customs, religion, and food, enriching American society and culture.

SEPARATE SPHERES

Women also endured discrimination. The idea of "separate spheres" held sway in this era—the belief that men were suited to the outside world of business and politics while women belonged to the domestic world of home and family. It was against this background that women fought for increased rights.

WOMEN OF COURAGE AND CONVICTION

ELIZABETH CADY STANTON (1815–1902)

Elizabeth Cady Stanton was a founder of the women's rights movement in the 1840s and remained committed to it until her death. Born in New York, she was educated at Troy Female Seminary. In 1840, she married Henry B. Stanton; the couple had seven children. During the Civil War, Elizabeth was active in the abolitionist movement. In 1869, she helped to set up the National Woman Suffrage Association and became its president. Elizabeth also lectured and wrote extensively. In 1890, she was named president of the new National American Woman Suffrage Association and held the post until 1892. She published *The Woman's Bible* (1895–98), in which she examined all the references to women in the Bible and showed how they had been interpreted in a way that was biased against women. She also helped to compile the first three volumes of the *History of Woman Suffrage* (1881, 1882, and 1887).

Left: Immigrants step off the boat at Ellis Island in New York in the late 19th century. It is estimated that nearly half of Americans today are descended from a family member who came to the country this way.

CHAPTER 2

WOMEN IN THE CIVIL WAR

Women's responsibilities during the Civil War increased enormously. In addition to caring for their families, they were left to supervise businesses and farms while the men were away fighting. Women also contributed to the war effort, collecting supplies for the troops and working as nurses, spies, and scouts. More than 3,000 women worked on both sides as nurses in difficult circumstances. So eager were women to contribute that an estimated four hundred women disguised themselves as men in order to serve as soldiers. This chapter examines the wartime experiences of three main groups of women: white women in the Union, white women in the Confederacy, and slaves and former slaves.

WOMEN OF COURAGE AND CONVICTION

MARY EDWARDS WALKER (1832–1919)

Mary Walker's father believed in the education of girls, and Mary was fortunate enough to attend Syracuse Medical College, graduating in 1855. With her husband, she set up a medical practice in New York, but it failed because few people were prepared to see a female doctor. When the Civil War broke out, women were not allowed to join the army, but Mary volunteered as a surgeon. She was appointed assistant surgeon in the Army of the Cumberland. In 1864, Confederate soldiers captured her as a spy and imprisoned her for four months. She was released in a prisoner exchange and returned to her duties as a surgeon for the rest of the war. In 1865, Mary Walker was awarded a Congressional Medal of Honor for Meritorious Service, the only woman to receive this honor.

Right: Dr. Mary Walker, who served as a surgeon during the Civil War

UNION WOMEN

Union women were more actively involved in the war effort than their Confederate counterparts. While the men were in the army, women took over jobs in factories, in government offices, in schools, and on farms. Of great assistance to the army were the Sanitary Commissions, organized by Dr. Elizabeth Blackwell. The 7,000 local chapters (groups) raised more than $50 million for the Union Army. They recruited nurses and provided food, clothing, and medical supplies.

Many women helped the commissions through voluntary work at home, sewing clothes for soldiers. They fund-raised for the army, donated items, and gave up their free time to help injured soldiers in hospital.

NURSES

Civil War nurses provided medical care, cooked meals, washed the patients, and cleaned the hospital wards. Some extraordinary women played a significant role in the nursing profession. Dorothea Dix

Left: Clara Barton tending wounded soldiers during the Civil War. She had special permission to go through the battle lines to bring supplies and nurse the wounded.

> ### A STRANGE DAY
>
> "I began my new life by seeing a poor man die at dawn, and sitting all day between a boy with pneumonia and a man shot through the lungs. A strange day, but I did my best; and when I put mother's little black shawl round the boy while he sat up panting for breath, he smiled and said, 'You are real motherly, ma'am.'"
>
> Writer Louisa May Alcott describes her first day working as a volunteer nurse for the Union army in December 1862.

devoted most of her life to improving the treatment of the mentally ill. During the war, she volunteered as the superintendent of Union nurses for the Sanitary Commission. Another courageous nurse, Clara Barton, risked her own life, going to the front lines to deliver supplies and nurse wounded soldiers.

CONFEDERATE WOMEN

Southern women faced more difficulties than those in the North. They were often forced to be involved in the war because the southern states were invaded and suffered devastation on a huge

WOMEN OF COURAGE AND CONVICTION

BELLE BOYD (1844–1900)

When the Civil War broke out, Virginia-born Belle Boyd undertook fund-raising activities to support the Confederacy. In July 1861, Union forces took control of her hometown of Martinsburg. Belle shot and killed a Union officer who attempted to enter her home to raise a flag over the house; she was acquitted (let off the charge) of murder. In the same year, Belle overheard that the army planned to destroy Front Royal's bridges when retreating from the town. She risked her life to travel across enemy lines to inform General Stonewall Jackson of the plan. After being arrested twice in 1862 and 1863 and serving prison sentences, in 1864 she sailed to England bearing letters from President Jefferson Davis to the British government. On the journey, she fell in love with a former Union officer, and the pair married in England. After her husband's untimely death in 1865, Belle returned to the United States.

Right: Buildings destroyed in Charleston, South Carolina, during the Civil War. Union forces blockaded the city from July 1863 to February 1865 and bombarded it, causing widespread damage.

scale. The South lost most of its male workforce: four out of five eligible men served in the army, while about half did so in the North.

Many women were left to run farms alone. The wives of slave owners had to manage the family's slave laborers, who were increasingly resentful of white control. As the war progressed, enslaved people grew hopeful of achieving freedom and were less inclined to follow orders. Also, they were used to receiving instructions from white men and did not necessarily respect the mistress's authority. As a result, southern farms became less productive during the war.

SHORTAGES AND HARDSHIP

Practical problems made white women's difficulties worse. There were severe shortages of food, clothing, and other goods, while high inflation raised the price of everything they had to buy. Spare parts for farm equipment were hard to find. In any case, women often lacked the knowledge to maintain the machinery.

Nevertheless, Confederate women participated in the war effort. As in the North, they sewed uniforms, donated food, and nursed wounded soldiers. Some women established private hospitals in their own homes or other buildings. Sally Louisa Tompkins set up a hospital in a donated building in Richmond, Virginia. When the Confederacy ordered the closure of private hospitals in September 1861, President Jefferson Davis made Tompkins a cavalry captain so she could maintain the hospital under military authority.

FIGHTING TO ABOLISH SLAVERY

During the Civil War, in 1863, the 13th Amendment was passed to free enslaved people in states "in rebellion against the United States"—that is, in the Confederate states. Both black and white women were involved in the

MANAGING THE SLAVES

"We are doing as best we know, or as good as we can get the Servants to do. . . . They seem to feel very indepenat [independent] as no white man comes to direct or look after them, for Willes speaks shorter to Johny and orders him about more than any negro on the place."

During the war, Georgia mistress Louticia Jackson ran a small plantation with the help of her teenage son Johny. She wrote in 1883 about the difficulty of managing the slaves, especially a man called Willes.

Right: This stained-glass window in St. James Episcopal Church in Richmond, Virginia, depicts Sally Tompkins with a medical bag, overseen by an angel.

WOMEN OF COURAGE AND CONVICTION

SOJOURNER TRUTH
(c. 1797–1883)

Sojourner Truth was the first black woman to speak out in public about slavery. Born a slave, she was freed in 1827. Believing that being an abolitionist was a duty to God, she began lecturing for the anti-slavery cause in 1846. In 1863, she went to Washington to help African Americans who had escaped from the South. After the Civil War, she campaigned for land to be offered to freed slaves in the western territories. Although Congress did not pass legislation as she requested, by the end of the 1860s, thousands of black people had fled the South to avoid racist violence and moved West. After the 15th Amendment gave the vote to black men but not to women, Sojourner lectured widely for the women's suffrage movement.

Right: Sojourner Truth financed her lecturing work by selling cards showing a photograph of herself, as explained in the caption (right).

I SELL THE SHADOW TO SUPPORT THE SUBSTANCE.

SOJOURNER TRUTH.

growing movement to abolish slavery altogether. For most, the issues of women's and black people's rights were linked in a struggle for equal rights for all.

Free black women campaigned in anti-slavery societies for abolition. However, it was hard for them to work with white women because the latter often did not treat black women equally. White women activists tended to exhibit the racism that was common at the time. Although they thought that slavery was an inhumane institution, most believed that African Americans were inferior to white people in their cultural development, intelligence, and behavior.

PREJUDICE

Black women suffered from disadvantages. Few had access to education, and they found it hard to publicize their views in the mostly white press. Just a handful of black women, such as Sojourner Truth and Sarah Parker Remond, were able to break through prejudice and broadcast their message to a wide audience. Sojourner worked in the United States, while Sarah moved to England in 1858 to gain support for the anti-slavery movement there.

In addition to campaigning for abolition, free black women gave practical help to slaves who escaped to Union lines during the war, providing them with food, clothing, medical supplies, and schoolbooks. The best known of these supporters was Harriet Tubman.

WHITE WOMEN ABOLITIONISTS

Although there were far fewer white women than men in the abolitionist movement, they undertook important work, campaigning

BREAKTHROUGH BIOGRAPHY

HARRIET TUBMAN (c. 1820–1913)

Harriet Tubman was born into slavery in Maryland. With the help of the Underground Railroad, a network of volunteers who helped to liberate slaves, she escaped to the North in 1849 and reached Philadelphia. She then made nineteen trips to the South to rescue about three hundred enslaved people. During the Civil War, Harriet worked for the Union Army as a nurse, cook, spy, and scout. Afterward, she became involved in the temperance and women's movements and helped to establish schools for newly freed people in North Carolina.

Below: Harriet Tubman, on the far left, photographed with slaves whom she helped to escape.

door to door and sending petitions to Congress. In 1863, they formed the National Woman's Loyal League to organize support for the total abolition of slavery; this helped to make it a national issue. Once slavery had ended, a number of female abolitionists continued as activists in the women's rights movement.

WOMEN AFTER THE CIVIL WAR

For four million enslaved people, the war brought freedom. Large numbers refused to return to work on plantations—they wanted independence. Without the resources to buy their own land, many turned to sharecropping—a landowner permitted them to farm a piece of land in return for a share of the crop. There were few job openings for black women in the South; the majority remained farm workers. Both women and men turned their attention to building family life.

Below: A female sharecropper works in a Georgia cotton field in 1870. The sharecropping system suited white planters because they did not have to pay wages. The African-American laborers had some independence but remained desperately poor.

TURNING POINT

THE ENDING OF SLAVERY

In 1865, the 13th Amendment to the Constitution of the United States abolished slavery. It was the first stage in the process of giving civil rights to African Americans. The text of the amendment stated: "Neither slavery nor involuntary servitude [forced slavery], except as a punishment for crime whereof the party shall have been duly convicted, shall exist within the United States, or any place subject to their jurisdiction [rule]. Congress shall have power to enforce this article by appropriate legislation."

"

FREE AT LAST

"Missus an' all was cryin', and say da catch Jeff. Davis [Jefferson Davis, leader of the Confederacy]. An' I hurried de supper on de table; an' I say, 'Missus, can Dilla wait on table till I go to de bush-spring an' git a bucket o' cool water?' She say, 'Hurry, Mill'; an' I seed 'em all down to table afore I starts. Den I walks slow till I git out o' sight, when I runn'd wid all my might till I git to de spring, an' look all 'round, an' I jump up an' scream, 'Glory, glory, hallelujah to Jesus! I's free!'"

In 1866, a Virginia woman spoke to an abolitionist about the experience of emancipation.

From 1865, former slaves were allowed to marry, and many couples did so. People made huge efforts to reunite families divided by slavery and the war.

EDUCATION

Before abolition, it had been illegal to teach slaves to read and write. In 1865, the Freedmen's Bureau was set up to provide practical assistance to former slaves, establishing one hundred hospitals and 4,000 schools. The bureau's greatest achievement was in education. It built Freedmen Schools, created teacher-training colleges, and provided teaching materials. Volunteers from churches and other organizations ran the schools. By 1876, there were 70,000 black people in school in the South, compared with none in 1860.

Nearly half of the teachers in the Freedmen Schools were women, both black and white. Conditions were hard: the salary was low, and the teachers endured harassment from whites who opposed the ending of slavery. The teachers stayed because they were committed to education and inspired by the enthusiasm of their students.

ECONOMIC PROBLEMS

For many white women in the South, the effects of the Civil War were less positive. Over half of the 800,000 men serving in the Confederate forces had been killed or badly wounded, and the conflict had caused the widespread destruction of property. Many wives were left widowed, and there was a shortage of younger men for women to marry. Women without support from a man were forced to take paid work. They labored in factories and on farms and as clerks and teachers. Some moved to northern cities to seek better jobs. Thus in both the North and the South, the Civil War forced black and white women into new roles, whether voluntarily or not.

Below: During the Civil War, men went off to fight and women filled vacancies in the factories. This photograph dates to around the 1890s; by then it had become more common for women to undertake factory work.

CHAPTER 3

HOME AND DAILY LIFE

EXCEPT FOR WEALTHY WOMEN WHO COULD AFFORD A TEAM OF servants, the majority of late-19th-century women and girls did a huge amount of housework every day. They also fed, clothed, nursed, and educated their families. If a woman ever got to sit down, she would be occupied mending or making clothes. Although all women's lives had much in common, their daily work differed, depending on their class, race, and location.

DAILY ROUTINES

An average day for an ordinary woman involved hauling in wood or coal to fuel the stove, and fetching containers of water for cooking and washing. She would then bake bread and cook meals on the stove, which needed continual attention. The stove gave out soot and dust, so she would need to clean and dust the rooms and furnishings daily. Doing the family's laundry could take an entire day. Once the clothes were dry, the woman would press them with an iron (made of cast iron) that had to be heated and was heavy to lift.

Below: A mother and her children pose for a photograph in about 1900. They are seated next to a spinning wheel the mother uses for work and the baby's wooden crib.

Above: In this advertisement dated 1882, a young man shows his wife a domestic sewing machine. The first sewing machines were produced in the 1830s and rapidly gained popularity.

RURAL WOMEN

Rural women's lives were even more exhausting than those of townswomen. They grew and made their own products, also creating goods for sale. Women spun thread to make cloth, grew food in gardens, and cared for animals such as chickens, producing food from them. They dried or salted surplus food to use in winter.

URBAN WOMEN

The rapid urbanization of the late 19th century led to great changes. In towns and cities, working-class families were usually crowded into tiny rooms in poorly maintained apartment buildings, often without running water. New immigrants, mostly from villages in southern and eastern Europe, flocked to the new cities. They had to adapt to

HOME, SWEET HOME

"Where is it that the eye brightens, the smile lights up . . . and every motion [is] cheerful and graceful? Is it at home? Is it in doing the work of the kitchen? Is it at the wash-tub—at the oven—darning a stocking—mending a coat—making a pudding? Is it in preparing a neat table and table cloth, with a few plain but neat dishes?"

In *The Young Wife* (1851), William Alcott gave an idealized view of a woman's duties in the home but left out any mention of the heaviest tasks.

A JEWISH IMMIGRANT

"I made $4 a week by working six days in the week. For there are two Sabbaths here—our own Sabbath, that comes on a Saturday, and the Christian Sabbath that comes on Sunday. It is against our law to work on our own Sabbath, so we work on their Sabbath.

In Poland I and my father and mother used to go to the synagogue on the Sabbath, but here the women don't go to the synagogue much, tho[ugh] the men do. They are shut up working hard all the week long and when the Sabbath comes they like to sleep long in bed and afterward they must go out where they can breathe the air. The rabbis are strict here, but not so strict as in the old country."

In 1899, thirteen-year-old Sadie Frowne came to the United States from Poland with her mother. She describes some of the ways that Jewish people adapted to life there.

Right: Seeking the New Home, a painting by Newell Convers Wyeth (1882–1945), gives an idealized view of new life in the West. In reality, settlers had to contend with droughts in summer, heavy snowfall in winter, and strong winds. They experienced shortages of water and wood.

BREAKTHROUGH BIOGRAPHY

ANNIE OAKLEY (1860–1926)

Born in Ohio, young Annie Oakley showed remarkable skill in using firearms, a traditionally male pursuit. She hunted game and at age fifteen won a shooting match with Frank E. Butler, a vaudeville marksman (he used his shooting skills as an entertainer). The pair were married, probably in 1876, and played in vaudeville circuses together. In 1885, Annie joined "Buffalo Bill" Cody's Wild West Show and became one of its star attractions. She toured with the show to Europe and was presented to Queen Victoria in 1887. Annie was injured in a train accident in 1901 but made a quick recovery and returned to the stage in 1902. She continued to exhibit her extraordinary skills as a markswoman for much of the rest of her life.

a different lifestyle. Women who were used to growing their own food now had to buy it. They learned to cook indoors on coal stoves instead of outdoors. A large proportion of the eastern European immigrants were Jews, escaping persecution. Although they had to adopt new ways, they also maintained their religion and customs.

THE WEST

The chance to build a new life extended to native-born Americans too. The development of the territories in the West from 1860 to 1880 offered white families economic opportunities. In 1862, the Homestead Act offered 160 acres of free land in the West to settlers who lived on it for five years. The experience for women pioneers in the West was mixed. Some loved their new environment, while others desperately missed their communities back east. Conditions for early settler women proved extremely tough. They helped construct their own homes and had to gather, grow, or make everything they needed to survive.

Bradley & Rulofson. *Sarah Winnemucca* San Francisco, Cal.

Above: A portrait of Sarah Winnemucca dating to around 1880. She was the first Native American woman to publish a book in the English language.

WOMEN OF COURAGE AND CONVICTION

SARAH WINNEMUCCA (c. 1844–91)

Sarah Winnemucca was born in the area that would later become the state of Nevada. Her father was chief of the Paiute nation. As a young woman, she converted to Christianity and adopted the name Sarah. In 1865, soldiers killed many Paiute in retaliation for the stealing of cattle; among the dead were Sarah's mother, sister, and baby brother.

Fluent in many languages, Sarah worked as an interpreter for the U.S. Army and from 1872 for her own people when they moved to the Paiute reservation in Oregon. In the early 1880s, she campaigned for the government to restore land to the Paiute. She went on a lecture tour, published a book, and circulated petitions, but her cause failed. From 1886 to 1889, she taught in Paiute schools; instead of the official European curriculum, she taught Indian history and culture.

NATIVE AMERICANS IN THE WEST

The westward expansion had a drastic effect on the domestic life of non-white populations. After the end of the Mexican–American War of 1848, the Southwest was ceded—handed over—to the Union. The United States did not recognize the land rights of the Native American people there; few groups were able to claim rights to their land successfully.

White settlers took over territory that had been held by Native American nations, forcing them to change their lifestyle. The presence of white people also altered gender relations. Before, Native American women and men had separate roles, but women were respected for their contribution to society. Men tended to be in charge of hunting,

BREAKTHROUGH BIOGRAPHY

SUSETTE LA FLESCHE (1854–1903)

Born into a prominent family in Omaha, Nebraska, Susette La Flesche received a European education at the mission school on her reservation. After completing her schooling at the Elizabeth Institute for Young Ladies in New Jersey, she returned to the Omaha Reservation to teach at a government school. In 1879, she gave evidence in court on behalf of the Ponca people. The Ponca had been forced to resettle in Indian Territory (now Oklahoma). They returned to Nebraska because of the miserable conditions in the Indian Territory and were arrested and put on trial. Owing to a strong defense, the court released them. Susette then went on a lecture tour to campaign for humane treatment, land rights, and citizenship for Native Americans. In 1881, she married Thomas H. Tibbles, a journalist who supported the Native Americans' cause, and the couple continued to work for Indian rights. Susette proved an inspiration for later human rights activists.

warfare, and interaction with people outside the group. Women were responsible for the home, children, household goods, and agriculture. The influence of European ways undermined respect for women. For example, white government agents saw women as inferior and would negotiate only with men. This treatment affected relations between Native American men and women; men became more dominant in Native American society.

As settlers took over the land, Native Americans were forced to move to reservations, where the land was usually poor and conditions were harsh. By 1880, most had been resettled. Between 1860 and 1880, over 33,000 Native Americans had died from starvation or disease.

MEXICAN WOMEN IN THE WEST

Mexican women had been migrating north for hundreds of years. Under Spanish and Mexican law, they held property rights. Once southwestern territory came under United States' control, American laws challenged these rights. Mexican women fought to keep control of their land, but by 1880, the amount of land they owned had declined greatly. Many Mexicans moved to *barrios* (Spanish-speaking areas) in large North American cities. Mexican women lost the independence that possessing land had given them and had to adapt to an urban lifestyle.

AFRICAN-AMERICAN WOMEN IN THE WEST

Although they formed a small minority of migrants, some African-American women joined the westward migration of the late 19th century, hoping to escape racism in the South. Many of them married and set up home with men who had previously moved west across the Great Plains to work as gold prospectors, railroad builders, or cattlemen.

MIDDLE-CLASS WOMEN

Well-off women, mostly white, had more advantages than Native American, Mexican, or African-American women, but

Left: A portrait of Susette La Flesche. As an outcome of the Ponca court case at which she gave evidence, Native Americans were recognized for the first time as human beings before the law. As human beings, they could not be imprisoned without just cause.

Above: This illustration shows women preparing an elaborate feast for Thanksgiving dinner in a big kitchen, around 1890. Middle-class families generally lived in large homes with many rooms.

their fate depended on their family. Owing to the popular notion of "separate spheres," men generally went out to work while women looked after the home. Some historians believe that industrialization caused this separation: it created jobs that paid wages mostly for men and left women in wealthy families completely dependent on the financial success of their husband. Others argue that better-off women enjoyed the shelter of the home. Staying home was a symbol of status that maintained class differences because working-class women had to go out to work.

CREATURE COMFORTS

Whether or not they were happy to stay home, domestic life became far more comfortable for middle-class women in the late 19th century. In this period, indoor plumbing was introduced, bringing hot and cold water directly to the home. In houses with piped water, women no longer had to fetch water every day or heat water to fill a large tub for bathing. The availability of electric lighting began to spread.

"

A WOMAN DEPENDS ON HER HUSBAND

"The working power of the mother has always been a prominent factor in human life. She is the worker par excellence [supreme], but her work is not such as to affect her economic status. Her living, all that she gets,—food, clothing, ornaments, amusements, luxuries,—these bear no relation to her power to produce wealth, to her services in the house, or to her motherhood. These things bear relation only to the man she marries, the man she depends on,—to how much he has and how much he is willing to give her."

Charlotte Perkins Gilman wrote about the unfairness of women's position as housewives in her book *Women and Economics* (1898).

Above: An 1870s advertisement for a domestic washing machine and wringer for squeezing out wet clothes. Early washing machines were operated by turning a handle.

TURNING POINT

INDOOR PLUMBING

In 1869, the Chicago Water Tower made history as the first system to supply water to a city in the United States. Steam engines drew water from Lake Michigan and pumped it into the city's water mains. Chicago also had the first complete sewerage system, designed in 1885. Many inventors worked to perfect the design of the water closet (flushing toilet). New homes began to be designed with a separate bathroom, containing a tub for bathing. The advent of indoor plumbing made a huge difference to women's and girls' lives.

Various labor-saving machines were invented, including the carpet sweeper, the washing machine, and the sewing machine.

By 1900, women could buy clothing made in factories. They could reduce the time they spent cooking by buying processed and canned foods. Heinz began producing canned foods in the 1870s, and in the following decade the first canned meals appeared. In the 1890s, Campbell's Soup Company started to make condensed soups. All these new inventions made life easier for middle-class women, whose families could afford them. These women found they had more free time to pursue interests outside the home.

CONTROLLING FAMILY SIZE

Women of all classes tried to improve their economic situation by limiting the number of babies they had and therefore the cost of raising a family. Reliable methods of birth control were not available, so abortion was the most common way to control fertility. The number of abortions soared between 1840 and 1880. Abortions were quite expensive and were mostly had by middle- or upper-class married, native-born Protestant women (Catholics believed abortion was wrong). Gradually, state lawmakers began to view abortion as a problem for society and introduced laws against it.

THE COMSTOCK LAW

Reformer Anthony Comstock campaigned enthusiastically for the passage of this law in 1873. It was intended to prohibit the mailing of indecent materials, including pornography and information about birth control or abortion—any material that was deemed at the time to encourage "immoral behavior." The effect was to censor the mail. If a post office inspector decided any item of mail was indecent, he seized all copies and would not deliver them. The Comstock Law severely limited the availability of information about birth control and abortion.

Right: A 1915 cartoon makes fun of reformer Anthony Comstock's campaign against immorality. It implies his views are so extreme that he would deem the birth of a naked child to be indecent.

MAIL RESTRICTIONS

"Sec. 148. That no obscene, lewd, or lascivious [lustful] book, pamphlet, picture, paper, print, or other publication of an indecent character, or any article or thing designed or intended for the prevention of conception or procuring of abortion, nor any article or thing intended or adapted for any indecent or immoral use or nature, nor any written or printed card, circular, book, pamphlet, advertisement, or notice of any kind giving information, directly or indirectly, where, or how, or of whom, or by what means either of the things before mentioned may be obtained or made . . . shall be carried in the mail."

An excerpt from the Comstock Law, 1873

"Your Honor, this woman gave birth to a naked child!"

CHAPTER 4

WOMEN WORKERS

Between 1870 and 1900, the proportion of women who worked for a wage increased from 14 to 21 percent. Most were young, poor, and single, and many of them were immigrants. The majority of women worked as servants or in manufacturing. Women had little choice over the type of work they did. It depended on their abilities to some extent, but in general, women undertook unskilled or semi-skilled work. Race and marital status (whether they were married or not) also affected the jobs available to women.

DOMESTIC WORK

Most women continued to work in traditional domestic jobs. Domestic workers, including household servants, laundresses, and waitresses, formed the largest category of female wage earners. In 1900, a quarter of women workers were servants. Usually done by African-

TURNING POINT

URBANIZATION AND INDUSTRIALIZATION

From 1870 to 1900, urban populations doubled every decade. By 1900, more than half of the U.S. population lived in towns and cities. People abandoned farms and flocked to urban areas to become wage laborers. At the same time, industrialization proceeded rapidly. Many different jobs were created in the industrial sector. Women often worked in the production of cloth, clothing, and food products. The female wage earner in the cities came to symbolize the rapid shift in the economy.

Left: Squatters in temporary housing in New York City, 1869. To accommodate the growing population, four-to-six-storey tenements were constructed to pack in the maximum number of tenants within the smallest space.

Above: A woman and four small girls work in their New York tenement home stringing flowers into wreaths to sell. Poor families needed to put their children to work to survive.

American or immigrant workers, domestic jobs had the lowest status. Many black women would have preferred other employment, but even if they were trained teachers or college educated, they were often rejected by potential employers because of their race.

WORKING AFTER MARRIAGE

Once married, white women stopped going out to work because it was seen as socially unacceptable. Yet extremely poor women—including black women all over the country and married Mexican women in the Southwest—had no choice but to continue in paid employment. In the late 19th century, poor married women of all races worked from home, often doing piecework. Entire families worked twelve to fourteen hours a day sewing or making small household items. It was badly paid and exhausting work. Women could also earn an income by cooking daily meals for single men or taking in boarders. Some ran taverns from home.

BLACK SERVANTS

"In answer to the schedule question, 'Have you ever tried to do other work?' a large number of domestics replied, 'I never go any place I'm not sure of—I won't give them a chance to refuse me.' One girl who had taught for four years and who thinks she lost her place at the end of that time from prejudice on the part of the school-committee, says, without the slightest apparent touch of resentment, 'The reason I don't try to teach is because I know I'd have trouble, and I can save as much this way.'"

In 1896, graduate student Isabel Eaton began a survey of black domestic servants in Philadelphia. They explained that it was hard to find any other types of work.

TURNING POINT

THE DAUGHTERS OF ST. CRISPIN

The first national organization of women workers, this union of shoe workers was formed in Lynn, Massachusetts, in 1869. The union demanded the same pay rates for women as for male laborers doing the same job. The Daughters of St. Crispin led two strikes in 1872, one of which achieved higher pay for women workers. The union lasted as a national organization until 1876.

Below: Women garment workers in the dressmaking department of a factory, around 1890. They worked in cramped, crowded conditions.

WORKING IN THE FIELDS

In rural areas, many black women worked as sharecroppers, as did some Native American and Mexican women. In white society, it was commonly believed that women were too frail to work in the fields and that this was black people's work. Yet in the South, although it was not their primary job, poor white women and girls undoubtedly worked in the fields alongside men and boys.

In addition to helping in the fields, rural white women produced food from their farms. In the mid-Atlantic states, they made butter and cheese, while in the South, women sold surplus garden produce, such as eggs and dairy products. Women also took on piecework alongside their children. Merchants provided them with raw materials to make goods such as hats, brooms, and cloth in their own home.

INDUSTRIAL WORKERS

From 1860 to 1880, white northern women found jobs in textile mills and in the clothing and cigar-making industries. Black women were generally excluded from all but the most menial industrial jobs. From 1880 onward, immigrant women and children entered jobs in factories and mills. Conditions in manufacturing were harsh: workers usually labored sixty to eighty hours a week in noisy, dangerous workplaces.

Above: A member of the Working Women's Protective Union listens to a female worker's complaint against a sewing machine dealer in the 1860s. The union tried to get women paid the agreed wage rather than fighting for increased wages.

Women earned far lower wages than men for the same work—but factory jobs paid much better than domestic employment.

THE LABOR MOVEMENT

As industrialization spread, labor unions sprang up to try to improve workers' conditions. They tended to exclude women, regarding them as competitors for jobs—although in fact men took most new jobs in manufacturing. An important exception was the Knights of Labor (KOL), formed in 1869 as a secret organization. Its aims included an eight-hour workday and equal pay for equal work. In 1879, it went public, forming local assemblies of working people. The KOL welcomed industrial workers of both sexes and, after 1883, African Americans. In 1886, it set up a women's branch, led by Leonora Barry. However, much of the labor movement did not accept all workers as equal. Strong anti-Chinese feelings existed among white working-class people. They contended that, because Chinese immigrants were prepared to work for low wages, they caused a decline in pay for all laborers. White women argued that they should be allowed to join unions alongside their male co-workers to resist the threat from Chinese labor. White workers of both sexes put pressure on the government to

> ## BREAKTHROUGH BIOGRAPHY
>
> ### LEONORA BARRY (1849–1930)
>
> Leonora Barry was born in Ireland and emigrated to New York with her parents in 1852. She became a teacher at age fifteen but had to resign when she married because only single women were allowed to teach. When her husband died in 1880, Leonora had to support her family. She took a job in a clothing factory and joined the women's branch of the Knights of Labor in 1884. Two years later, Leonora was elected to lead the branch, the first woman to become a paid labor organizer. An individual with great energy and enthusiasm, she traveled around the country persuading women to join labor unions and campaigning for better working conditions. Leonora resigned in 1890, by which time the KOL was in decline.

WOMEN OF COURAGE AND CONVICTION

MARY HARRIS JONES (1830–1930)

Known as "Mother Jones," Mary Harris came to the United States from Ireland as a child. In 1867, her husband and four children all died of yellow fever. Disaster hit again in 1871 when her dressmaking business was destroyed in a fire. Mary then became an organizer for the KOL, urging on the miners during their 1874–75 strike in Pennsylvania. During the 1880s, she fought for the eight-hour workday, returning to union activity in 1891 when she became an organizer for the United Mine Workers. When miners in Pennsylvania went on strike in 1899–1900, she coordinated the miners' wives to support them. The workers won the strike and received a wage increase. Afterward, Mother Jones campaigned to end child labor. She continued to struggle for workers' rights for the rest of her life, believing working-class protest was more important than women's right to vote.

restrict Chinese immigrants. In 1882, a law was introduced to prevent Chinese laborers from entering the country, and other laws followed during the 1880s and 1890s.

INDUSTRY IN RURAL AREAS

The labor movement was active in the countryside. In rural areas, entire families, including young children, worked in mills or mining camps six days a week. Conditions were hazardous and uncomfortable, while wages barely covered rent and the basic necessities of life. Young children regularly suffered physical harm, losing fingers in machinery or suffering backaches from carrying heavy loads. Labor leaders such as Mary Harris Jones focused their efforts on improving conditions and banning child labor.

NEW JOBS IN STORES AND OFFICES

Meanwhile, native-born white women with some skills could enter new white-collar jobs. Previously the office had been a male domain. Typewriters were invented in the 1860s and by 1890 were commonly used in businesses. The invention led to an explosion of secretarial and clerical jobs, deemed suitable for women. The introduction of the telephone in 1876 transformed communications—by 1890, there were more than 250,000 telephones in the United States. Thousands of

Below: The typing pool at the National Cash Register Company, Dayton, Ohio, around 1902. Its owner, John Henry Patterson, treated his women workers well, providing chairs with backs for support and offering soup and coffee for lunch.

INDEPENDENT WOMEN

"There is nothing in clerical training that detracts from [lessens] the finest womanly qualities, and men have outgrown their admiration for feminine helplessness and have come to look upon independence as something worth having. Clerical training educates the mind to accuracy in details, punctuality in the daily affairs of life, economy in the adjustment of time, and quickness of perception [understanding]. Perhaps this is the reason why so many men choose a wife amid the deft-fingered clerks in preference to the society misses."

In 1891, journalist Clara Lanza responded to critics of female office workers, declaring that they were reliable and exhibited high moral standards and that the training made them good wives.

Left: A teacher and student in a one-room schoolhouse in Ohio, around 1900. It was acceptable for young women to work as schoolteachers or as governesses teaching the children of one family.

women were employed as telephone operators. By 1900, women formed 75 percent of office staff. Women also took jobs as sales clerks in retail stores.

Some people did not think that female office workers should be hired. Male critics argued that women were too temperamental, lacked concentration, and were not capable of working steadily. They also claimed that office work made women unsuitable for marriage and child rearing. But these criticisms did not stem the tide of change.

WOMEN IN THE PROFESSIONS

Just a few openings existed for well-educated women in the late 19th century. Of all the professions, teaching was the one in which women

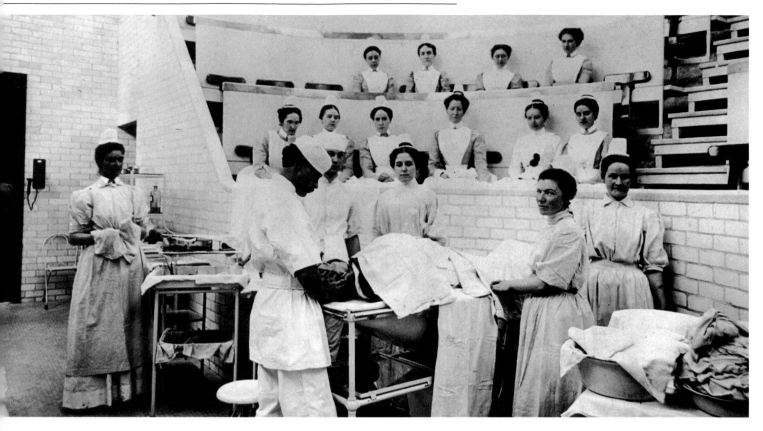

Above: Nurse interns watch from a gallery as a surgeon and nurses prepare to perform an operation in an amphitheater in a hospital in New York City in 1899.

WOMEN OF COURAGE AND CONVICTION

BELVA LOCKWOOD (1830–1917)

Belva Lockwood taught school from age fifteen until her marriage. After her husband died in 1853, she returned to teaching to support herself and her daughter. She also continued her own education, determined to become a lawyer. Three colleges refused her application to study law, but she was finally admitted to the National University Law School. In 1873, she graduated and was admitted to the District of Columbia Bar. However, as a woman, she was not allowed to speak before the Supreme Court. Belva then introduced a bill to allow female lawyers to practice in federal courts. It was eventually passed in 1879, and Belva was the first woman permitted to speak before the Supreme Court.

were most likely to be employed. Before the Civil War, most teachers were male. By 1890, 72 percent of teachers were female. Other women achieved careers as writers, or artists. Yet it remained hard for women to break into fields such as science, architecture, medicine, or law.

MEDICINE AND LAW

As the 19th century progressed, physicians increasingly required a medical degree to practice. Since women had less access to higher education than men, it was harder for them to become doctors. In addition, discrimination prevented women from attending medical school alongside men. Separate medical schools for women were established; there were seven of these by the late 19th century. In 1890, about 5 percent of doctors in the United States were women. Nursing was considered a woman's job, but no official training existed until three nursing schools were established in 1873.

The legal profession was also extremely reluctant to admit women. In 1890, only 208 American women were working lawyers. Early female lawyers learned their skills through apprenticeship to family members in the profession rather than by going to law school.

AFRICAN-AMERICAN PROFESSIONALS

As in the white community, the proportion of female African-American teachers grew during the late 19th century. African-American women also taught in black colleges and teacher-training institutes in the South. Access to the medical profession was limited for African-American women. Few hospital training schools admitted black trainee nurses. In 1886, the first black nurses' training program was set up at Spelman Seminary. Black women belonging to social clubs, and doctors, founded additional schools in the 1890s. Yet graduates found it hard to get jobs owing to racism on the part of employers, and they received less money than white nurses for the same work. From the 1860s, a few black women graduated from women's medical schools. In 1890, there were 115 African-American women physicians.

BUSINESSWOMEN

Some women took an independent route to a career by setting up companies. A few successfully turned the concerns of the "women's sphere" into business opportunities. For instance, cook and nutritionist Fannie Farmer promoted healthy meals and wrote the best-selling *Boston Cooking-School Cook Book*.

BREAKTHROUGH BIOGRAPHY

MARTHA MATILDA HARPER (1857–1950)

Martha Harper worked from childhood as a domestic servant. Through her own research, she discovered how to use herbs to improve the hair and skin. In 1888, she founded her first hair salon in Rochester, New York. It was a new concept—in those days, women cared for their hair at home. Well-off visitors to the city soon discovered the merits of her treatments. Three years later, Martha founded the chain Harper Hair Dressing Salons with salons in different cities. She ensured that all her treatments contained safe, organic substances; every salon used the same techniques and products. Martha employed working-class women to run the salons—they were often former servants, who understood customer service. In this way, ordinary women were able to acquire their own businesses and prosper independently.

Left: Fannie Farmer with one of her students at Miss Farmer's Boston cooking school. Fannie Farmer made cooking easier by using a system of level measurements in her recipes so that the dishes turned out right every time.

CHAPTER 5

THE STRUGGLE FOR SUFFRAGE

FOLLOWING THE ABOLITION OF SLAVERY, WOMEN ACTIVISTS FOCUSED on their own rights. Women generally had more rights in the new western states: in most states they could own property and keep their own wages. The first states to allow women to vote were in the West, including Wyoming in 1869 and Utah in 1870. In the late 19th century, women built a campaign for the right to vote throughout the United States.

A CIVILIZING INFLUENCE

"'Manhood suffrage,' or a man's government, is civil, religious, and social disorganization. The male element is a destructive force, stern, selfish, aggrandizing [appearing powerful], loving war, violence, conquest, acquisition, breeding in the material and moral world alike discord, disorder, disease, and death. . . . The strong, natural characteristics of womanhood are repressed and ignored in dependence, for so long as man feeds woman she will try to please the giver and adapt herself to his condition. . . . The need of this hour is not territory, gold mines, railroads, or specie payments but a new evangel [gospel] of womanhood, to exalt [honor] purity, virtue, morality, true religion, to lift man up into the higher realms [levels] of thought and action."

In a speech given to the Woman's Suffrage Convention in 1868, Elizabeth Cady Stanton urged the passage of a 16th amendment that would give women the right to vote.

WOMAN SUFFRAGE IN WYOMING TERRITORY.—SCENE AT THE POLLS IN CHEYENNE.

Above: Women vote in Wyoming in 1870; this was the first election in which women could vote after the passage of the state's 1869 suffrage law.

Above: Elizabeth Cady Stanton discusses a document with Susan B. Anthony, who is standing next to her.

SUSAN B. ANTHONY (1820–1906)

Brought up in the Quaker tradition, Susan Anthony was encouraged to be independent. As a young woman, she became a teacher and in the 1850s joined the temperance and anti-slavery movements. During the 1860s, she began to work with Elizabeth Cady Stanton, and from 1868 to 1870, she acted as the publisher of the weekly journal the *Revolution*, which demanded equal rights for women. A founding member of National Woman Suffrage Association, Susan traveled extensively to lecture on the need for women's suffrage. In 1872, she voted illegally in the presidential election in Rochester, New York. She was arrested, tried, and ordered to pay a fine, which she refused to do. Susan was president of National American Woman Suffrage Association, the merged women's suffrage movement, from 1892 to 1900.

CHANGES TO THE LAW

The 14th and 15th amendments had a huge impact on the campaign for the right to vote. The 14th Amendment gave equal rights to all citizens, while the 15th Amendment allowed black men to vote; voters were defined in the law as males. The discussions over the 15th Amendment in the late 1860s caused a division among women activists. Some, such as Elizabeth Cady Stanton, believed they should not support the 15th Amendment unless women as well as black men gained the vote. Others, including Lucy Stone, thought that giving African-American men the vote was a good first step, which would make it easier to argue that suffrage should be extended to women too. In 1869, two organizations were formed, reflecting the two different opinions: National Woman Suffrage Association (NWSA) and American Woman Suffrage Association (AWSA).

NATIONAL WOMAN SUFFRAGE ASSOCIATION

Led by Elizabeth Cady Stanton, Susan B. Anthony, and Sojourner Truth, NWSA was larger and more radical than AWSA. Its main aim was to amend the U.S. Constitution to give women the vote, but it

WOMEN OF COURAGE AND CONVICTION

LUCY STONE (1818–93)

Lucy Stone's father was a farmer who did not believe in educating his daughter. However, Lucy was determined to achieve academic success. While working as a teacher, she saved up enough money to attend Oberlin College. After graduating, she became a lecturer for the abolitionist movement. Once slavery was abolished, she threw herself into the women's rights campaign, helping to found AWSA in 1869. The following year, she established the weekly *Woman's Journal*; she and her husband, Henry Blackwell, became its editors in 1872. The newspaper was one of Lucy's major contributions to the suffrage movement. In the late 1880s, she was influential in healing the rift between the two suffrage organizations. When they merged in 1890 to become National American Woman Suffrage Association, she became the executive chairperson. Lucy continued to work for women's rights until her death.

Right: The platform of the NWSA convention in Chicago, 1880. At the annual conventions, the organization hammered out its policies through debate and discussion. Gradually, the suffragists widened their influence in society.

also campaigned on other women's rights issues, such as the unfair divorce laws. In the early days, there was great public opposition to NWSA's stand from both men and women.

AMERICAN WOMAN SUFFRAGE ASSOCIATION

AWSA was founded by Lucy Stone and her husband, Henry Blackwell, as a more moderate alternative to NWSA. AWSA focused on attaining suffrage on a state-by-state basis: it put pressure on individual states to give the vote to women. The organization avoided involvement in other women's rights issues and concentrated on suffrage alone.

Like NWSA activists, AWSA members organized local groups and held public meetings to air their views and build up political support. They drew up petitions, gave lectures, wrote letters, produced publications, and lobbied the lawmakers of individual states to give women the vote.

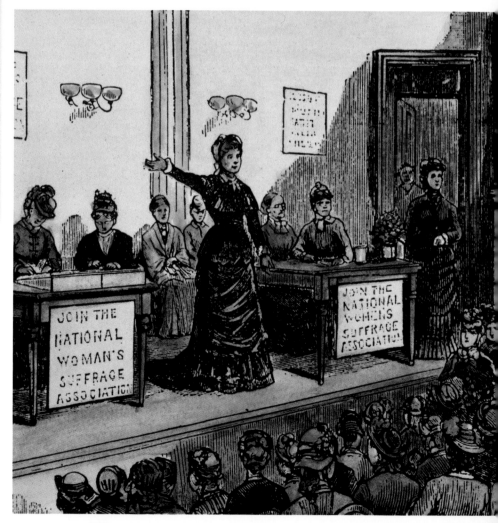

WORKING WOMEN AND SUFFRAGE

While AWSA placed pressure on lawmakers, NWSA tried to broaden support for women's rights in society. In 1868, Susan B. Anthony and Elizabeth Cady Stanton encouraged New York women to set up working women's associations in an attempt to mobilize working-class women wage earners and involve them in the struggle for suffrage. The suffragists linked the demand for equal pay for equal work to the demand for the vote. Many women workers were interested in having the vote, although not all. Some thought that women's loyalty should lie with the labor movement, alongside working-class men, and that suffrage was not a priority. It proved hard to attract working-class women to the suffrage cause.

BLACK WOMEN AND THE SUFFRAGE MOVEMENT

While working-class women were divided about women's suffrage, in general black people favored universal suffrage—the vote for all. Black women's clubs promoted the suffrage cause in their

CONFLICTING VIEWS

"*I contemplate with joy the future, and look forward to the 'good time coming' . . . when woman shall have her rights and all professions shall be open to her as a man; when she shall occupy positions which males occupy now, but which rightly belong to her; and hope soon woman's voice shall echo in senate chambers and halls of representatives.*"

"*Heaven help us! if the time has come when we can no longer place confidence in our fathers. . . . It will be a bitter and humiliating day for me when I take the ballot from the hand that is left to me, to smooth the rough places in life; for that day will bring with it a conviction that the judgment I rely on has failed me.*"

The first quote, by Ella A. Little, and the second, by a woman writing under the pen name "Americus," show how the opinions of skilled working women differed in regard to female suffrage. Both women were members of the Daughters of St. Crispin.

Left: A portrait of Julia Ward Howe, a wealthy Boston woman who helped to found the New England Women's Club in 1868. She was well known for having written "Battle Hymn of the Republic," the most popular song of the Civil War. After attending a lecture by Lucy Stone at the club, she became convinced of the justice of the women's suffrage cause and helped to form AWSA the following year.

FOR AND AGAINST

"JACOB
*I don't believe a single bit
In those new-fangled ways
Of women running to the polls
And voting nowadays. . . .*

JOHN
*Now, Jacob, I don't think like you;
I think that Betsy Ann [Jacob's wife]
Has just as good a right to vote
As you or any man. . . ."*

The arguments for and against women's suffrage are outlined in a poem by Frances Ellen Harper, which was published in a New York African-American journal in 1885.

Right: Frances Ellen Harper, who supported the 15th Amendment to give the vote to African-American men as a step toward equal rights. She could see no reason for "Black women to put a single straw in the way to prevent the progress of Black men."

community as well as improved rights for African Americans. The National Association of Colored Women (NACW) focused on issues such as child care and equal pay for equal work; it also had a suffrage department. Important activists included Frances Ellen Harper, who had helped Lucy Stone to found AWSA. Josephine Ruffin was active in mainly white Boston clubs that aimed to achieve social and political empowerment for women. In 1890, she established the first African-American women's newspaper, *Woman's Era*, and in 1893 the mostly black Woman's Era Club, which called on black women to fight for increased civil rights for their people.

VICTORIA WOODHULL

In addition to organized groups, some strong-minded individuals became involved in the women's suffrage movement. Victoria Woodhull argued that women fit the conditions of citizenship as mentioned in the 15th Amendment: "privileges of citizenship can not be denied on

Left: This political cartoon from an edition of *Harper's Weekly* from 1872 has the caption "Get Thee Behind Me Mrs. Satan." It depicts Victoria Woodhull as a demon for promoting the cause of "free love," which was seen as immoral.

> ### BREAKTHROUGH BIOGRAPHY
>
> #### HARRIOT STANTON BLATCH (1856–1940)
>
> The daughter of Elizabeth Cady Stanton, Harriot Stanton was educated at Vassar College. She became involved in the women's suffrage movement in 1882, writing a chapter in the *History of Woman Suffrage*, which her mother and Susan B. Anthony were compiling. She ensured that the activities of their rivals in AWSA were included. In the same year, she and her husband moved to England, but Harriot remained involved with the movement. Some historians credit her with helping to reconcile differences between AWSA and NWSA in 1890. In 1902, she and her family returned to the United States, where she injected energy and determination into the suffrage movement and made great efforts to include working-class women.

account of race, color, or previous condition of servitude." On this basis, Woodhull bravely ran for the presidency in 1872 as the candidate for the Equal Rights Party. She held some more controversial views. She did not believe that people should have to marry and stay with one partner all their lives but that men and women should be free to love different people. Most people in the women's rights movement felt that Woodhull's views were outrageous and would harm their plea for suffrage, so they distanced themselves from her.

MOVING TOWARD UNITY

By the late 1880s, the divisions among suffragists had diminished. The 1888 International Congress of Women brought together delegates from AWSA and NWSA in a joint effort to build the women's movement internationally. It featured about eighty speakers

TURNING POINT

THE NAWSA CONVENTION

On the first day of a convention held in Washington, D.C., in February 1890, AWSA and NWSA were formally merged to create the National American Woman Suffrage Association (NAWSA). The leading activists from AWSA and NWSA took up major positions in NAWSA. Elizabeth Cady Stanton was elected president, although having just celebrated her seventieth birthday, she clearly would not be heavily involved. Susan B. Anthony was named vice president and would run the organization, while Lucy Stone became chair of the executive committee. In her presidential address, Elizabeth urged the women in the new organization to be attentive not only to their own needs but also to those of women of different religions and races as well as immigrants.

Above: In 1873, NWSA presented a petition to Congress for the right of women to vote. The signatures of Susan Anthony, Matilda Gage, and Elizabeth Cady Stanton are visible at the bottom.

from around the world. Important male supporters were present too, including Lucy Stone's husband, Henry Blackwell, and Frederick Douglass. At the conference, the older generation of activists encouraged younger women to work together to achieve equal rights for women.

NATIONAL AMERICAN WOMAN SUFFRAGE ASSOCIATION

In 1889, leading members of NWSA and AWSA signed a document titled "Open Letter to the Women of America," declaring they would "work in harmony with all other Associations of like character—and as in union there is strength." In 1890, the two organizations merged to form the National American Woman Suffrage Association (NAWSA). Other organizations, such as the Women's Christian Temperance Union, joined the campaign for women's suffrage.

ANTI-SUFFRAGE SOCIETIES

As the movement for women's suffrage grew, so did opposition to it. The first group was the Woman's Anti-Suffrage Association of Washington, D.C., formed in 1870 by some wealthy women, including Mrs. William Sherman (wife of a famous Union general) and Mrs. John Dahlgren. In 1882, Boston women set up the Boston Committee of Remonstrants (protesters).

Anti-suffragists argued that men adequately represented the women in their household. If women had the vote, they might challenge the view of male family members and threaten their authority. Some said that politics was a dirty world full of plotting and intrigue; by becoming involved in it, women's "purity" would be spoiled. It was also claimed that women had no desire to vote and would not know how to use this power. From a religious perspective, it was argued that allowing women the vote was against God's law.

Anti-suffrage societies used tactics similar to suffragists. They organized petitions, published pamphlets, wrote letters to the press, and gave public lectures. They put their case to state lawmakers to try to prevent them from approving female suffrage.

By 1900, the women's suffrage movement was making progress, despite opposition. Women could hold meetings in prestigious public venues and make speeches that would be reported favorably in the press. Although they had not yet achieved their goal, they had attained respect. The younger generation of women would continue the struggle.

Right: Anti-suffrage societies continued their opposition to the vote for women after 1900; this photo dates to 1915.

DABBLING DISCONTENTS

"Of all the shrill complainers that vex [irritate] the ears of mortals there are none so foolish as the women who have discovered that the Founders of our Republic left their work half finished, and that the better half remains for them to do. While more practical and sensible women are trying to put their kitchens, nurseries, and drawing-rooms in order, and to clothe themselves rationally, this class of Discontents are dabbling in the gravest national and economic questions."

Novelist Amelia Barr was one of the few women who attacked women's suffrage in print. In this 1896 article, she shows her scorn for women who want to become involved in politics.

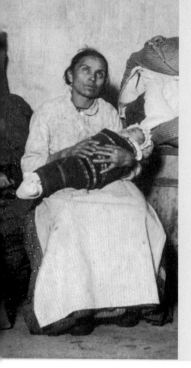

CHAPTER 6

WOMEN'S NATIONAL ASSOCIATIONS

ROM THE 1860S, WOMEN'S ASSOCIATIONS BECAME extremely important for middle-class women, both black and white. Millions of women joined clubs relating to their interests outside the home. These new women's organizations were national and led solely by women. The most significant were the temperance groups and women's clubs. There were also movements to improve life for poor people in cities, including settlement houses to help immigrants.

TEMPERANCE MOVEMENT

The temperance movement—the campaign against the production and sale of alcoholic drinks—had emerged in the early 19th century, but it experienced a great surge after the end of the Civil War. Activists saw alcoholism as a serious threat to society. Unlike the suffrage movement, the temperance campaign was seen as a respectable activity for females and was far more popular among women. In 1873, the Women's Temperance Crusade was formed. Female church members entered saloons, praying and singing hymns and begging saloon keepers to stop selling liquor. The crusade spread to twenty-three states, and thousands of saloons were forced to close down.

Members of the crusade discussed the need for a national campaign, which led to the establishment in November 1874 of the

Left: Temperance activists pray outside a New York tavern in 1874 as drinkers look on. The women of Fredonia, New York, were the first women's group to visit saloons in this way.

Above: This cartoon depicts a temperance crusader, dressed like a medieval knight, slashing open casks of liquor "in the name of God and Humanity."

WOMEN OF COURAGE AND CONVICTION

FRANCES E. WILLARD (1839–98)

A teacher by profession, in 1873 Frances Willard took on the senior position of dean of women at Northwestern University. The following year, she became secretary of the WCTU and served as its president from 1879 till her death. Willard argued that alcoholism was the result of poverty rather than its cause, a radical view at the time. She expanded the scope of the temperance movement to deal with wider issues, too. Society defined women as homemakers, so Frances argued that to protect their home, women should be involved in matters that affected their families. She organized campaigns on several issues under the banner of "home protection," including the reform of the child labor law, child care, and women's suffrage. In 1879, she published *The Home Protection Manual*, a guide for local temperance unions, and in 1883 founded a world temperance union.

DEMON DRINK

"When I passed the saloon-keeper's house, I saw his wife . . . and she was dressed in silks and laces. . . . 'Your money helped to buy the silks and laces, and the horses and carriage. . . . I come here and I find your wife in a faded calico [cotton cloth] gown, doing her own work; if she goes any where, she must walk. . . . You love the saloon-keeper better than you love yourself.'"

Mary Clement Leavitt, a leading member of the WCTU, spoke in 1888 about how she confronted an alcoholic who was destroying his family and persuaded him to mend his ways.

Women's Christian Temperance Union (WCTU) in Cleveland, Ohio. Its first president was Annie Wittenmyer and the second, Frances E. Willard. The WCTU grew rapidly both in the North and the South, working to spread its message through schools, churches, and other organizations.

The temperance movement soon became linked to the wider movement for women's rights. In 1876, Willard began to argue that women's suffrage was necessary to achieve the goals of the

WOMEN OF COURAGE AND CONVICTION

CARRIE NATION (1846–1911)

In her early adulthood, Carrie Nation witnessed the problems caused by liquor firsthand. In 1867, she married Charles Gloyd, an alcoholic, whom she soon abandoned. She was remarried in 1877 to a much older man, but this marriage was also unhappy. She joined the WCTU in 1890, when a U.S. Supreme Court decision weakened the Prohibition law in Kansas, where she lived. Although liquor was illegal in Kansas, it could be imported from other states and sold in its "original package." Many illegal saloons sold liquor. Either alone or with other women, Carrie began to march into saloons, singing and praying, and then proceeded to smash up the furnishings with hatchets. Carrie was jailed several times for these attacks and was herself physically assaulted. She lectured frequently for the temperance movement and also supported women's right to vote.

Right: A montage of Christian Science churches in the United States, with a photo of Mary Baker Eddy at the top, from the *Illustrated London News* in 1906. Although the church is described as a "superstition" in the article, it is clear that it has become extremely popular.

temperance movement. Then women would have a voice in matters concerning the liquor trade in their area. In 1878, the WCTU collected 180,000 signatures on a petition to Illinois State requesting local suffrage for women. In 1890, the WCTU became part of the National Woman Suffrage Association.

THE CHURCH OF CHRIST, SCIENTIST

The women's temperance movement arose from strongly held Christian beliefs. One woman, Mary Baker Eddy, found that her religious ideas did not fit with the churches of the time. Therefore in 1879 in Boston, Massachusetts, she founded her own, the Church of Christ, Scientist, which combined a faith in the healing power

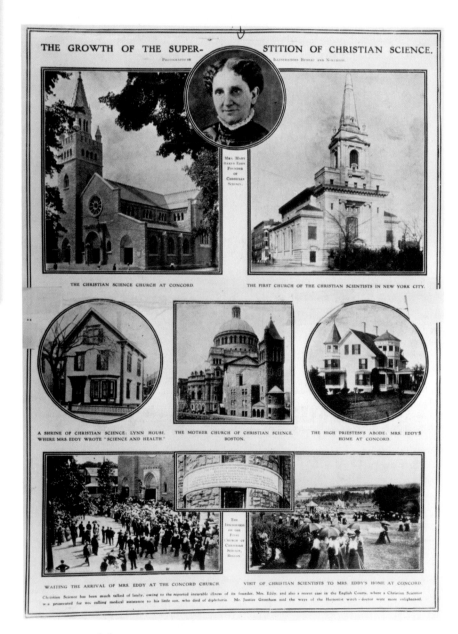

of God's love with Christianity. It was extremely rare for a woman to establish a religious movement.

WOMEN'S CLUB MOVEMENT

The women's club movement was another significant development in the late 19th century. It was first and foremost a movement of middle-class women who had time to spare. Initially the clubs focused on the self-education of their members, often meeting to discuss literary themes. They tended to broaden to encompass a range of issues. Some club members joined the suffrage movement. The majority of women's clubs became involved in social reform, although they retained their concern with women's self-education and advancement. The club movement expanded greatly in the 1880s and 1890s, reaching all areas of the country and a variety of communities. In 1890, the General Federation of Women's Clubs was formed; it had one million white women members. All the clubs were involved in meetings and public speaking and held annual conventions.

Most women's organizations were split on racial lines. Black women were rarely permitted to join white women's clubs, so they organized

AT THE EMANCIPATED WOMEN'S CLUB.

BREAKTHROUGH BIOGRAPHY

MARY BAKER EDDY (1821–1910)

Mary Eddy's early life was harsh. She was seriously ill as a child, her brother died when she was twenty, and she became a widow at twenty-two after just six months of marriage. After her second marriage, she was separated from her only child. In the 1860s, she turned to theories of spiritual healing and became convinced that illness came from the mind. In 1879, she founded the Church of Christ, Scientist, which incorporated healing into religious practice. The church rapidly gained followers, known as Christian Scientists, in the United States and other countries. In addition to acting outside traditional female roles in her own life, Mary supported women's suffrage and property rights.

Left: This satirical cartoon from *Puck* magazine, 1896, plays on the fear that the women's rights and suffrage movements would lead mothers to abandon their families. A child brings a message to her mother, who is relaxing at the Emancipated Women's Club, to tell her about an important moment in family life. The father is caring for the children—unheard of in those days.

45

WOMEN OF COURAGE AND CONVICTION

IDA B. WELLS-BARNETT (1862–1931)

The daughter of enslaved parents, Ida Wells-Barnett was determined to fight against the racial segregation introduced in the southern states after the end of slavery. In 1884, she was forced to move to the "colored" car on a train. Outraged, she sued the railroad company, and incredibly, she won. After losing her teaching job in 1891 for writing articles criticizing the schooling available to African-American children, she bought a partnership in the African-American newspaper *Free Speech* and turned to journalism. Ida began to campaign against lynching, for which she was attacked by racists. Her newspaper office was set on fire and she received death threats. Yet Ida continued her work, and her courageous efforts led to an anti-lynching campaign involving African Americans and some white people. The campaign spread, and gradually during the 1890s, southern states introduced anti-lynching laws.

Above: This 1901 cartoon shows that lynching black people destroys justice itself—represented by the woman holding the scales of justice being burned at the stake. "Judge Lynch" was a term for the unauthorized punishment of criminals by lynching.

separate movements. For example, Mary Church Terrell founded the National Association of Colored Women in 1896. Within nine years, it had a membership of 50,000.

Black and white groups worked in their own communities in areas such as education, child care, public health, temperance, and suffrage. In addition, the black club movement hoped to combat racial prejudice and improve the position of African-American people in general.

NATIVE AMERICAN REFORM MOVEMENT

Native Americans developed their own reform movement in the late 19th century. Indian women took up the struggle to preserve their culture and identity, and the right to their own tribal government. An important figure was Zitkala-Sa, born in 1876 to a Sioux mother and an Anglo-American father. At age eight, she was sent to a boarding school for Native Americans, where the children were forced to adopt a Western way of life. This inspired her to fight to prevent Native American children from being removed from their homes and culture.

IMPROVING THE CITIES

Some organizations aimed to improve conditions in urban areas. Middle-class women formed working girls' clubs to help young female laborers and to try to promote middle-class values. The general public expressed great concern about the new generation of young female workers in cities, many of whom lived away from their families in overcrowded boardinghouses and labored long hours. Various associations were founded to address their difficulties. For instance, the

Below: A shop assistant at the canned goods counter at Macy's Department Store, New York City, around 1898. Store jobs appeared attractive but in fact involved hard work and long hours.

THE SCRAMBLE FOR WORK

"That she must be on her feet most of the day and work for $1.50 or at most $2.00 a week, and may not be counted worth more than this for two or three years, does not deter hundreds from applying if any vacancy occurs. . . . If wages are a pittance [very low], hours exhausting, and an army always waiting to fill their places if they in any way forfeit them [give them up], the fact of companionship and of the constant interest and excitement of watching the throng in shop and street seems sufficient to satisfy all longings and prevent much complaint."

Reformer Helen Campbell investigated urban poverty in the 1880s and 1890s. In this excerpt from one of her books, published in 1893, she discusses the hard work and low pay of sales clerks in New York.

"

LIVING AMONG THE POOR

"In spite of some untoward experiences, we were constantly impressed with the uniform kindness and courtesy we received. Perhaps these first days laid the simple human foundations which are certainly essential for continuous living among the poor: first, genuine preference for residence in an industrial quarter to any other part of the city, because it is interesting and makes the human appeal; and second, the conviction, in the words of Canon Barnett, that the things which make men alike are finer and better than the things that keep them apart."

Jane Addams talked about the establishment of Hull-House in her book *First Days at Hull-House*, published in 1910.

National Consumers League was established in 1899 to try to better the situation of women working in department stores.

THE SETTLEMENT MOVEMENT

Another scheme that aimed to raise urban living standards was the settlement movement. Inspired by a similar project in London, in 1889 Jane Addams and Ellen Gates Starr moved into an old mansion in a Chicago slum and offered help to underprivileged white immigrants in the area. Educated young women came to offer their services, providing a day nursery to care for children while their mothers worked, teaching English, and running cultural classes to help incorporate the immigrants into American life. Called Hull-House, this was the first settlement house in the United States.

The settlement movement rapidly spread around the United States. In 1889, College Settlement was opened in New York City in a community of east European Jewish and German immigrants. The settlement was run by female graduates of Smith, Vassar, and Wellesley colleges. By the mid-1890s, it ran a kindergarten and library, offered

Below: This 1887 photo shows an Italian immigrant ragpicker with her baby in a small run-down tenement room in New York City. Immigrants generally lived in impoverished conditions, and their home was often their workplace.

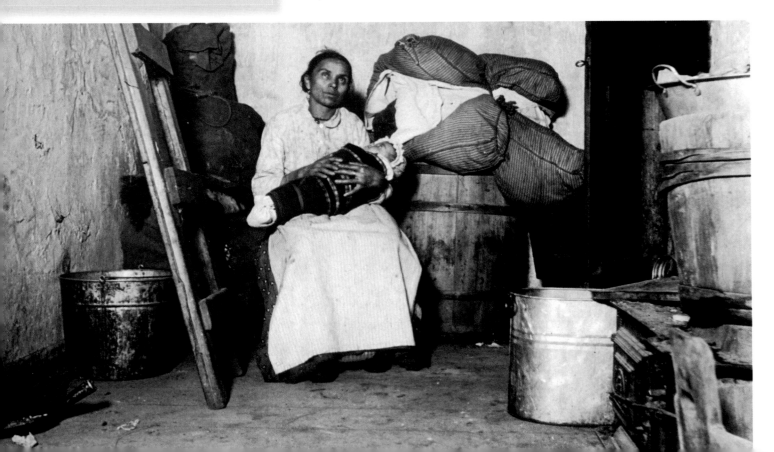

practical classes in sewing and crafts, and courses in literature and history. By 1900, there were 100 settlements around the United States; approximately half of the major ones were led and staffed mainly by women.

FIGHTING FOR REFORM

Yet the settlement pioneers were not only concerned with offering practical assistance. During the 1890s, they also campaigned to amend the laws that regulated immigrants' lives. They fought for child labor reform and the regulation of tenement housing and helped to organize labor unions. They protested about sweatshops—the cramped, uncomfortable, dirty, and dangerous places where many immigrants labored for long hours each day.

AFRICAN-AMERICAN SETTLEMENT HOUSES

African-American churches joined the settlement movement. They founded houses in the North to help newly arrived migrants from the South by providing employment, education, and welfare services. These migrants were not served by the white settlement houses, which helped to integrate white European immigrants into the community but not black people. Black women were active in the movement. In addition to assisting migrants, they worked tirelessly to improve the rundown neighborhoods where settlements were located, campaigning for better lighting, sewer systems, and garbage collection.

TURNING POINT

ILLINOIS FACTORY INSPECTION LAW

In 1893, this groundbreaking law in Illinois banned the labor of children under age fourteen. It also limited the working hours of women and people under eighteen to eight hours a day, outlawed the production of clothes in tenements, and created a state factory inspection office. The law was passed after intense pressure from Hull-House residents and other well-known Chicago women. A leading campaigner, Florence Kelley, had drafted the law and was subsequently appointed chief factory inspector of Illinois. It was extraordinary for a woman to hold such a position: she was responsible for the labor legislation of the entire industrial region of Illinois! However, the Illinois Supreme Court of 1895 overturned the law, and women's organizations had to continue the fight for shorter working hours.

Left: This image from the 1913 Hull-House Yearbook is entitled "At the Door of Hull-House." A worker from the house welcomes an immigrant woman and her small children.

CHAPTER 7

EDUCATION, LITERATURE, AND THE MEDIA

Most states did not make it compulsory for children to go to school until the late 19th and early 20th centuries. Middle-class girls, whose families could afford to educate them, usually attended private schools. During the late 19th century, many public high schools were opened, and by 1900, there were marginally more public secondary schools than private ones. Despite this, most poor girls had to work to help support their families. Their only chance of education was to learn from others in the family or to teach themselves.

Above: This classroom photograph from 1900 shows girls learning to sew and cook while the boys on the left practice woodwork.

AFRICAN-AMERICAN EDUCATION

In 1860, even free black people had few educational opportunities or institutions. Enslaved people gained the right to education only when they were liberated. After the Civil War, Freedmen's Schools offered schooling for the newly freed slaves. Urban African Americans in particular—both men and women—proved eager to learn. In 1865, 95 percent of southern black people could not read or write. By 1890, the figure had dropped to 64 percent.

In the 1870s, local and state governments in the South began to take responsibility for providing public elementary schooling for both white and black children, in segregated schools. Compared to the schools for white pupils, African-American schools were overcrowded and poorly equipped.

NATIVE AMERICANS

Native Americans were also educated in segregated institutions. In the 1870s, the Bureau of Indian Affairs set up boarding schools. The students were forced to abandon their own ways and adopt Western customs, which the teachers claimed were superior. Native American girls were taught their place within the "woman's sphere." They learned how to cook, sew, clean, wash clothes, and manage a home so that they would grow up to be efficient housekeepers. Cut off from their families, the girls often felt desperately lonely, and once they returned to their reservations, many found it hard to adjust back to their own society.

Below: A white teacher with a class of Native American students at the Carlisle Indian School, Pennsylvania, around 1900. Its founder, Richard Pratt, described his aim to "kill the Indian in him [the student], and save the man."

ANXIOUS TO IMPROVE

"In my own day school and night school, I have 140 pupils, who have made truly wonderful progress. . . . I find the people here more tidy and thrifty than in any place I am acquainted with—though many are intensely poor—and there had been nothing given them from the North, they are always tidy, cheerful and hopeful, ever anxious to improve."

Sarah and Lucy Chase were white Quakers who taught in the South during the Civil War and stayed to teach in Freedmen's Schools until 1869. Sarah wrote this letter to a friend at the New England Freedmen's Aid Society in 1866.

TURNING POINT

HIGHER EDUCATION FOR WOMEN

After the Civil War, women increasingly sought entry to higher education. Colleges began to admit women, and the proportion of female students leapt from 21 percent in 1870 to 35 percent in 1900. Given that women still suffered a high level of discrimination in society, these figures are remarkable. However, it is important to remember that few people, either male or female, went into higher education at the time. In 1870, 1 percent of college-age people went to college; even by 1900, the figure was just 4 percent.

Above: College students do experiments and make calculations during a physics class in around 1900. By this date, several women's colleges had proved that women had the intellectual capacity to study science.

LIMITED EQUALITY

"As a colored girl, I was accorded the same treatment at Oberlin College at that time as a white girl under similar circumstances. Outward manifestations of prejudice against colored students would not have been tolerated for one minute by those in authority at the time. . . . Although for many years there was as much 'social equality' to the square inch in Oberlin College as could be practiced anywhere in the United States, I have heard the authorities state that there had never been a case of intermarriage between the races in the whole history of the school."

Mary Church Terrell was one of two black students in her class when she attended Oberlin College in the 1880s. Although she did not suffer from prejudice, it was made clear that there should be no racial mixing outside school.

WOMEN'S COLLEGES

The number of colleges as well as schools expanded in the late 1800s, including the establishment of several new women's colleges. Vassar Female College opened its doors in 1865, offering high-quality education equivalent to that of the top men's colleges, such as Yale and Harvard.

Founded by Sophia Smith in 1871, Smith College was a private liberal arts college for women. In 1875, Wellesley College opened. All but one of the seven professors and fourteen teachers were women. Bryn Mawr, founded in 1885, offered women the chance to do original research and was the first college to offer PhD programs to female students.

Women could also go to "annexes" of elite male universities. Several universities welcomed women students, including Iowa, Wisconsin, Missouri, Michigan, and California. Coed institutions became more popular than single-sex colleges. By 1900, twice the number of women went to coed institutions as attended single-sex ones.

Left: Mary Church Terrell, who graduated from Oberlin College in 1884, went on to work as a teacher, although her father believed it was wrong for her to have a job.

BLACK WOMEN AT COLLEGE

Some schools, for example, Antioch and Oberlin, accepted a few black students. In the 1860s and 1870s, northern missionaries founded the first colleges for African Americans, including Howard University, in Washington, D.C., in 1867. Open to all races, the university's goal was to provide advanced education for black students.

EDUCATION IN THE SOUTH

New institutions were also opened in the South. Missionaries, northern philanthropists, and African-American communities supported private secondary schools and colleges that provided a liberal arts education. One of these was Spelman Female Seminary in Atlanta, Georgia. In the 1890s, the southern states began to provide public higher education for black people—mostly agricultural, technical, and teacher training colleges. Except for the Atlanta Baptist Female Seminary, African-American colleges were coed.

> ### BREAKTHROUGH BIOGRAPHY
>
> #### SOPHIA B. PACKARD (1824–91)
>
> Born in New Salem, Massachusetts, Sophia Packard worked as a teacher for many years. In 1880, she toured the South and decided to set up a school for African-American girls and women. The following year, she and her companion Harriet E. Giles founded the Atlanta Baptist Female Seminary in a church basement in Atlanta, Georgia. The two women taught in the school and organized prayer meetings and Sunday schools. Enthusiastic students flocked there: within a year, 150 women had enrolled, and, by the end of 1883, numbers had increased to four hundred. The students were mainly middle-aged former slaves, eager to gain an education. In 1883, the school moved to a permanent site. Wealthy industrialist John D. Rockefeller was so impressed by Packard's project that, in 1884, he paid off the balance due on the building. Sophia continued to help run the school until her death.

AN INSPIRATIONAL WRITER

"She did not think herself a genius by any means; but when the writing fit came on, she gave herself up to it with entire abandon, and led a blissful life, unconscious of want, care, or bad weather, while she sat safe and happy in an imaginary world, full of friends almost as real and dear to her as any in the flesh. Sleep forsook her eyes, meals stood untasted, day and night were all too short to enjoy the happiness which blessed her only at such times."

One of the characters in Louisa M. Alcott's novel *Little Women* is Jo, a creative young woman who has time and space for her writing work. Jo provided great inspiration to many female readers, who traditionally did not have such freedom.

OPPOSITION TO FEMALE EDUCATION

Some people strongly opposed the expansion of higher education for women. In 1873, Dr. Edward Clarke published *Sex in Education*, in which he argued that higher education was too taxing for young women, caused mental health problems, and made them unable to have babies. However, students, reformers, and women professionals strongly disagreed. In the 1890s, a new criticism arose—that higher education limited a woman's chance of marriage. Surveys showed that less than half of female graduates married and that those who did tended to marry later and have fewer children. In fact, the same was true of male graduates, but this caused less concern.

Interestingly, members of the wealthiest families in American society were indeed worried that a college education could make their daughters unmarriageable. Thus most white women at college between the 1860s and 1890s came from relatively well-off Protestant families—but not the elite.

Below: The wealthy young women shown in this 1866 painting *The Croquet Game* would be expected to engage in ladylike pastimes such as sewing, croquet, and music, and to find a rich husband. Attending college was not on the agenda.

LITERATURE

The debates about women in higher education affected only a minority of American women. It was rare for girls even to go to high school, much less college. Self-education was therefore of great importance. Women read books and magazines and wrote letters and diaries. In the 1860s, the market for young people's books became divided by gender. A new demand arose for books that appealed to girls, in contrast with the exciting adventure stories for boys. *Little Women*, by Louisa May Alcott (1869), proved very popular among middle-class girls and young women, including African Americans. It describes the different experiences of four sisters growing up in a modest New England family.

Other successful women writers included Emily Dickinson, whose numerous poems elaborated on themes such as God, life, nature, and friendship—and, when many of her loved ones died, the topic of death.

> ▶ **BREAKTHROUGH BIOGRAPHY**
>
> **EMMA LAZARUS (1849–87)**
>
> Emma Lazarus, who was descended from Jewish immigrants, received a good private education. Her first book of poems was published when she was only eighteen, and she wrote several other poetry volumes. During the early 1880s, news of the persecution of the Jews in Russia greatly affected her, and she started to write prose pieces to generate sympathy for the Jewish people. She took up the cause of Zionism, the call for the creation of a Jewish homeland in Palestine. In 1883, Emma's poem "The New Colossus" was selected to be inscribed on the base of the Statue of Liberty. The final lines are: "Send these, the homeless, tempest-tost to me, / I lift my lamp beside the golden door!"

Left: Poet Emily Dickinson preferred her own company, and led a secluded life at home. However, she corresponded with others to develop her creativity. She wrote 1,775 poems, only ten of which were published during her lifetime.

Above: This image of people bicycling on Riverside Drive, New York City, in 1895 is a sign of the times. Along with the men are several "New Women" enjoying this carefree pastime, albeit in ladylike clothing.

WOMEN OF COURAGE AND CONVICTION

CHARLOTTE PERKINS GILMAN (1860–1935)

Charlotte Perkins Gilman was born in Hartford, Connecticut. Her father abandoned the family, and she grew up in poverty. She received little formal education but taught herself through reading and became an art teacher. After an unhappy marriage to another artist, she was divorced in 1884. Charlotte became interested in socialist ideas and also wrote a volume of poetry. In 1898, she published *Women and Economics*, which became her best-known work. Here she expressed her belief that women could achieve equality only when they earned their own wage. She encouraged women to become professionals and skilled workers rather than enduring a domestic life. Charlotte suggested the establishment of day-care centers for children to enable women to do this. Women who could afford it would pay for domestic services, such as cooking, to give them time to devote to their job. Charlotte's ideas were revolutionary at the time.

THE MEDIA AND WOMEN'S RIGHTS

Certain women writers dedicated their energies toward the struggle for women's rights. New women's publications appeared, including the *Revolution*, a newspaper set up by Elizabeth Cady Stanton and Pillsbury Parker in 1868. It covered a wide range of issues, including female suffrage, religion, marriage, divorce, and the struggles of working women to gain equal pay for equal work. The newspaper reflected the growing influence of women in public life.

At the end of the 19th century, the struggle to reform women's rights began to broaden out to a more general belief that women were equal to men. It was simply that society denied them the chance to progress in life in the same way. Writer Charlotte Perkins Gilman suggested that equal involvement in the economy would allow them to do this.

THE NEW WOMAN

The developments in women's rights led to the emergence of the "New Woman" of the 1890s. A term coined by journalists, the New Woman was likely to be college educated, single, and independent. If she decided to marry, she would want a small family and to continue an active life outside the home.

New women were not only white. Black educator Anna J. Cooper expressed the open-minded and independent spirit of the New Woman. Born to an enslaved mother, in the 1880s Anna was one of the first African-American women to receive a degree. She became a teacher and writer, publishing *A Voice From the South* in 1892, in which she considered the problem of racism in the white women's movement and sexism in the African-American community.

Left: Educator Anna J. Cooper, the only woman elected to the American Negro Academy, a group of black scholars established in 1897.

"

OBSTACLES TO FEMALE EDUCATION

"I was asked a few years ago by a white friend, 'How is it that the men of your race seem to outstrip the women in mental attainment?' 'Oh,' I said, 'so far as it is true, the men, I suppose, from the life they lead, gain more by contact; and so far as it is only apparent, I think the women are more quiet. They don't feel called to mount a barrel and harangue [rant] by the hour every time they imagine they have produced an idea.'

But I am sure there is another reason which I did not at that time see fit to give. The atmosphere, the standards, the requirements of our little world do not afford any special stimulus to female development."

In this quote from *A Voice From the South*, Anna J. Cooper tries to understand why African-American women are held back from high educational achievement.

CHAPTER 8

THE PERIOD IN BRIEF

BY 1900, MARRIED WOMEN HAD THE RIGHT TO CONTROL THEIR OWN property and earnings. Better-off women could take advantage of new innovations that made their domestic lives easier. Yet for many working-class women, home life was as exhausting as ever. Large numbers had to adapt to a new life in cities or as immigrants to the United States. Native American women who had been forced to move to reservations had to adjust to the loss of both their livelihood and respect for their role within the community. Generally, African-American women still endured racism and poverty, but their situation was better in the North than in the South.

Below: Members of a Blackfeet Native American family sit outside their tepee on the Blackfeet Indian Reservation on the Great Plains, Montana, in 1887. During that decade, many of the Blackfeet starved to death owing to the near extinction of the buffalo, on which they depended for food.

WORKING LIFE

A few women in 1900 enjoyed professional careers as doctors, lawyers, or writers. More were able to become teachers and nurses. Industrialization allowed many women to work outside the home in factories. Women had some involvement in the growing labor movement. Yet businesses did not pay women as much as men.

WOMEN'S ORGANIZATIONS

Women had proved themselves to be capable organizers: and they controlled their own associations, independently of men. The large women's social reform movement had been accepted by society: both the temperance and settlement movements were influential. African-American women's groups had developed in parallel to white organizations, working for similar social reforms. The women's suffrage movement had made great strides. By 1900, there was more support in society for women's suffrage than in 1860. Yet the vote for women would not be achieved for another two decades.

THE BEGINNING OF FEMINISM

At the very end of the 19th century, the strength of women's organizations led to the beginnings of feminism. New thinking about women's economic role had emerged as well as the desire for equality with men—ideas that would develop rapidly in the new century.

Below: An African-American church congregation in Washington, D.C., in the 1870s. Life was less harsh for African Americans in the North than in the South.

59

THE KINDER NORTH

"I've lived all ma' life he'er in de South but ef I could'da gone north when I wuz young, I'd lacked [liked] it bedder [better], see deres mo' to be seen up dere. People is kinder up dere, dey call dat God's Country. Ain't no Mistrus's an' Marsters up dere. . . . When I wuz up dere wid ma' fo'ks, dey say, 'Now mama, a'ter ya cross de Mason-Dixie Line [the line dividing the North from the South], all de pe'ple is de same up he'er.' No gwin in de back door. . . . De white fo'ks up dere wuz so kind to me, I didn't know how to take it."

Sarah Fitzpatrick, born in Alabama in 1847, was an African-American house servant until she was freed after the Civil War. Later she visited her relatives in the North and described the difference there.

TURNING POINT

A LANDMARK FOR FEMINISM

In 1899, Kate Chopin published her second novel, *The Awakening*. Kate gives a sympathetic portrayal of her heroine, Edna Pointellier, who gradually discovers that she is bored with her life as a wife and mother and falls in love with another man. Edna's great passion and independence of thought shine through the novel—although she is never able to be with the man she loves. *The Awakening* proved shocking at the time and was little read until it was rediscovered in the 1960s. It then received praise as a landmark work that examined the concerns of the feminist movement of the 20th century.

TIMELINE

1860–80	Many Native Americans are forced to leave their land and are resettled elsewhere.
1861–65	The Civil War is fought.
1862	The Homestead Act offers 160 acres of free land to settlers in the West who live on it for five years.
1863	The National Woman's Loyal League is formed to campaign for the total abolition of slavery. The 13th Amendment frees enslaved people in the Confederate states.
1864	Abraham Lincoln is re-elected as president.
1865	The 13th Amendment abolishes slavery throughout the United States. President Lincoln is assassinated. Reconstruction begins; government is re-established over the whole country.
1868	Elizabeth Cady Stanton and Pillsbury Parker set up the *Revolution*, a women's rights newspaper. The 14th Amendment gives African-American people citizenship and equal legal and civil rights. *Little Women* is published.
1869	The National Woman Suffrage Association and American Woman Suffrage Association are set up. The Daughters of St. Crispin, a union of women workers, is formed in Lynn, Massachusetts. Wyoming is the first state to allow women to vote and to hold office.
1870	Lucy Stone sets up the *Woman's Journal*. The first anti-suffrage organization, the Woman's Anti-Suffrage Association of Washington, D.C., is formed. The 15th Amendment states that voting rights cannot be denied because of race, color, or former slave status.
1870s	The Bureau of Indian Affairs sets up boarding schools for Native Americans.
1873–78	An economic depression takes place.
1872	Victoria Woodhull becomes the first woman to run for the presidency. Susan B. Anthony and thirteen other women vote in the presidential election in Rochester, New York, and are arrested.
1873	The Women's Temperance Crusade is formed and spreads to twenty-three states. Dr. Edward Clarke publishes *Sex in Education*, in which he argues that higher education is too taxing for young women. The Comstock Law prohibits the mailing of "indecent materials," including pornography and information about birth control and abortion.
1874	The Women's Christian Temperance Union is founded in Cleveland, Ohio.
1877	Reconstruction collapses; southern states start to bring in laws that discriminate against African Americans.

1879   An act is passed allowing women attorneys to practice in federal courts.
        Frances Willard's *Home Protection Manual* is published.
        Mary Baker Eddy founds the Church of Christ, Scientist.

1880–1900   More than nine million people migrate to the United States.

1881   The Atlanta Baptist Female Seminary is founded in Atlanta, Georgia.
        Clara Barton forms the American Red Cross.

1883   Frances Willard founds a world temperance union.
        Emma Lazarus writes "The New Colossus," the poem that is inscribed at the base of the Statue of Liberty.

1886   The Knights of Labor set up a women's department, led by Leonora Barry.

1888   The International Congress of Women is held in an attempt to build the women's movement internationally.

1889   Jane Addams and Ellen Gates Starr establish the first "settlement house" in a Chicago slum.

1890s   The "New Woman" emerges.
        The southern states begin to provide public higher education for black people.

1890   The two rival suffrage organizations, NWSA and AWSA, unite to form the National American Woman Suffrage Association.
        The General Federation of Women's Clubs is formed.
        Josephine Ruffin founds the *Woman's Era*, the first African-American women's newspaper.

1893   Josephine Ruffin founds the Woman's Era Club.
        The Inspection Law bans child labor and limits the working hours of women and minors to eight hours a day.
        New Zealand grants suffrage to women.

1895   Elizabeth Cady Stanton publishes *The Woman's Bible*.

1896   The National Association of Colored Women (NACW) is established.

1898   Charlotte Perkins Gilman's book *Women and Economics* is published.
        The United States defeats Spain in the Spanish–American War and annexes (takes control of) the Philippines, Guam, and Puerto Rico.
        The United States annexes Hawaii.
        Britain conquers Sudan.
        Marie Curie discovers radium.

1899   Kate Chopin's novel *The Awakening* is published.
        The National Consumers League is set up to encourage women to use their power as consumers and to campaign for improved working conditions for women workers.

Glossary and Further Information

abolitionist Someone who fought to end slavery.

abortion The deliberate ending of a pregnancy.

apprenticeship Working for someone for a period of time to learn skills.

Bar The legal profession.

birth control Controlling the number of children a person has.

boardinghouse A house that rents rooms and provides meals.

boom A period when the economy is doing well.

censor To prevent certain types of information from being distributed.

citizenship The legal right to belong to a particular country.

compulsory Something that must be done by law.

Confederacy The states that left the Union in 1860.

constitution A set of laws governing a country or organization.

depression A period when the economy is doing badly and many people are out of work.

discrimination Treating a particular group in society unfairly, for example, because of their race or gender.

empowerment Giving people more control over their life or the situation they are in.

executive Having the power to put important decisions into effect.

immigrant A person who moves to settle in another country.

Industrial Revolution The period in the 19th century in the United States when machines began to be used to do work and industry grew rapidly.

inflation A general rise in the prices of goods and services in a country.

labor union An organization of workers that exists to protect their interests and improve their working conditions.

lynching When a group of people capture someone they believe has committed a crime and kill the person illegally.

mission school School run by missionaries, people who aim to spread Christianity.

persecution Treating people badly, for example, because of their race, religion, or political beliefs.

petition A written document, signed by a large number of people, that asks somebody in a position of authority to do or change something.

philanthropist A rich person who helps the poor, for example, by giving money to set up a school or another institution.

piecework Work that is paid for by the amount done rather than by the hours worked.

pioneer One of the first people to go to live and work in a particular area.

plantation A large area of land where crops are grown.

pornography Books or other media that describe or show naked people and sexual acts, usually in a way that many people find offensive.

prejudice Negative feelings toward a group of people that are not based on facts.

Prohibition Forbidding by law the making or selling of liquor.

Quaker A member of a Christian religious group that is opposed to violence. The Quakers were against slavery.

racism Unfair treatment or violent behavior toward people of a different race.

radical Extreme.

Reconstruction The process during which government was re-established over the entire United States and new laws were introduced. It took place from 1865 to 1877.

reservation An area of land designated for Native Americans to live on.

revolutionary Involving a complete change.

segregation The policy of separating people of different races (or religions or sexes) and treating them differently.

sewer system A system to carry away waste from homes and businesses.

sexism The unfair treatment of people, especially women, because of their gender.

socialist A person who believes that everyone has an equal right to a share in a country's wealth.

specie payments When the banks give the value of paper money in gold coins.

spiritual healing Using natural healing energy to help to cure a person.

strike When workers refuse to work, as a protest.

suffrage The right to vote in political elections.

suffragist A person who campaigns for the right to vote in political elections.

surplus An amount that is extra or more than a person or country needs.

sweatshop A place where people work for long hours in poor conditions for low wages.

temperance Not drinking liquor because of moral or religious beliefs.

tenement A large building divided into apartments, especially in a poor area of a city.

Union The northern states that remained under Abraham Lincoln's government when the southern states left in 1860 to form the Confederacy.

urbanization A process in which more and more people move from the countryside to cities.

white-collar jobs Jobs in offices rather than factories.

BOOKS

Crompton, Samuel Willard. *Clara Barton: Humanitarian.* New York: Chelsea House, 2009.

Currie, Stephen. *Women of the Civil War.* San Diego, California: Lucent Books, 2003.

Frost, Elizabeth, and Kathryn Cullen-Dupont. *Women's Suffrage in America.* New York: Facts On File, 2005.

Horn, Geoffrey Michael. *Harriet Tubman: Conductor on the Underground Railroad.* New York: Crabtree, 2009.

Keating, Susan. *Women of the West.* Broomall, Pennsylvania: Mason Crest Publishers, 2007.

Kudlinski, Kathleen V., and Lenny Wooden. *Sojourner Truth: Voice for Freedom.* New York: Aladdin Paperbacks, 2003.

Lantier, Patricia. *Harriet Beecher Stowe: The Voice of Humanity in White America.* New York: Crabtree, 2009.

MacDonald, Fiona. *Women in History: 19th Century America.* London, UK: Chrysalis Children's Books, 2003.

Moore, Heidi. *Elizabeth Cady Stanton.* Oxford, UK: Heinemann, 2004.

Moore, Heidi. *Ida B. Wells-Barnett.* Oxford, UK: Heinemann, 2004.

Sonneborn, Liz. *Women of the American West.* Danbury, Connecticut: Children's Press, 2005.

Stein, R. Conrad. *Harriet Tubman: On My Underground Railroad I Never Ran My Train Off the Track.* Berkeley Heights, New Jersey: Enslow, 2010.

WEB SITES

http://americancivilwar.com/women/women.html

http://b-womeninamericanhistory19.blogspot.com

www.chesapeake.edu/library/EDU_101/eduhist_19thC.asp

www.42explore2.com/suffrage.htm

www.pbs.org/wgbh/amex/oakley/timeline/index.html

FEB 2012